The

T0167888

CAROLINE BIRD is a poet and playwright. She has five previous collections of poetry published by Carcanet. Her most recent collection, *In These Days of Prohibition*, was shortlisted for the 2017 T.S. Eliot Prize and the Ted Hughes Award. A two-time winner of the Foyle Young Poets Award, her first collection *Looking Through Letterboxes* was published in 2002 when she was 15. She won an Eric Gregory Award in 2002 and was shortlisted for the Geoffrey Dearmer Prize in 2001 and the Dylan Thomas Prize in 2008 and 2010. She was shortlisted for Most Promising New Playwright at the Off-West-End Awards, and was a finalist for the Susan Smith Blackburn Prize. Her theatre credits include: *The Trojan Women* (Gate Theatre, 2012), *The Trial of Dennis the Menace* (Purcell Room, 2012), *Chamber Piece* (Lyric Hammersmith, 2013), *The Wonderful Wizard of Oz* (Northern Stage, 2015), and *The Iphigenia Quartet* (Gate Theatre, 2016). She was one of the five official poets at the 2012 London Olympics.

Also by Caroline Bird from Carcanet

CAROLINE BIRD

The Air Year

C △ R C △ N E T

First published in Great Britain in 2020 by
Carcanet Press Ltd
Alliance House, 30 Cross Street
Manchester M2 7AQ
www.carcanet.co.uk

A CIP catalogue record for this book is available from the British Library

ISBN 978 1 78410 902 8

The publisher acknowledges financial assistance from Arts Council England

Typeset in England by XL Publishing Services, Exmouth
Printed and bound in England by SRP Ltd, Exeter

'In the middle of the forest there's an unexpected clearing
that can only be found by those who have gotten lost'.

– Tomas Tranströmer (trans. Robert Bly)

Contents

Mid-air

There is a corner of the city where the air is
soft resin. Step in and it hardens
around you. Suspended
in amber. We made
the mistake of kissing there. I mean, here.
Our mouths midway
across the same
inhalation like robbers mid-leap between
rooftops. If kisses were scored by composers
they'd place the breath on the upbeat. Oh
God. Music preceded by mid-air,
when the baton lifts, the orchestra tightens: 'And'
before the 'one two three.' And
the sunlight is meticulous. And the river
holds its tongue. And your silver
earring steels like an aerialist's hoop, caught
mid-spin. A note almost sung. Locked
in the amber of the and.
We just want to land or
be landed on.

Dive Bar

Through a red door down a steep flight
of stairs into a windowless cellar
with sweating walls
an ingénue in a smoking jacket
sits atop a piano
as a host of swaying women
sing 'Your Secret's Safe with Me'
and one invites you
into the privacy of a kiss – all these
dark clandestine places – and you find
yourself imagining a very tiny
woman walking straight
into her mouth
through a red door down a steep flight
of throat into a windowless cell
with breathing walls
an ingénue in a smoke jacket
sits astride a piano
as a host of swallowed women
sing 'Your Secret's in a Safe,'
the barmaid shakes a custom
cocktail she calls 'A Private Kiss'– all these
dark half-eaten faces – and you find
yourself imagining a tiny tiny
woman walking straight
into her mouth
through a red breath down a dark
thought into a swallowed sense
with shrinking walls
an innuendo in stomach acid
slops upon a piano
as a host of silent passions
mouth 'Your Secret is Yourself'
inside the belly of the world – all these
dark dissolving spaces – and you find

yourself imagining a windowless
woman breaking
walls down in herself, sprinting
up the shrinking
halls and up contracting
corridors and up the choking
fits of hard stares through dark
thoughts and dead
laws through the red door
as it swallows shut behind you
now you're spat out
on the pavement with
the sun just
coming out.

Nancy and the Torpedo

Nancy found an entire torpedo in the forest
just lying there like a beached whale,
coated in wet leaves
and decorated with glittering snail trails.
'It's a fucking torpedo,' she said.

'Is it... live?' I said.
I didn't know how torpedoes worked.
Were they like mines?

'It's inert,' she said, suddenly an expert,
'torpedoes don't explode on land,
everyone knows that.' She whistled like a plumber
surveying a damp patch, 'He's a beauty alright.
I reckon he weighs at least 600 pounds. 640, I'd say.'

'He?' I said, but Nancy was already straddling it,
spanking its rudder like the rump of a prize horse.
'What's a torpedo doing in a forest?'

Nancy rolled her eyes.
'You always ask the most obvious questions, don't you?
Can't you just enjoy the moment?'

She'd already unzipped her trousers
and was touching herself, grinding up
against the girth of the weapon
and groaning gently. 'Careful,' I said.

Her orgasm gathered to a scream.
She pressed her sweating face
on the warhead and fell asleep on top of it.
The torpedo precisely matched the length of her body.

To my tired gaze, it seemed
as if they were *both* breathing,
Nancy and the torpedo, their chests
rising and falling together
like unsuspecting ocean waves.

I pictured them both in action,
underwater, Nancy's legs wrapped around
its speeding shaft, her red eyes fixed like sniper
dots on the target ahead, a string of bubbles
flying out behind her like a chiffon scarf.

Eventually she woke, refreshed and cheerful,
patted the torpedo goodbye, hoisted on her backpack
and we continued our journey
as if nothing had happened.

'Where are we going?' she'd ask, every ten minutes or so.
'We've just got to keep moving,' I'd reply, pointing
in some arbitrary direction and striding with purpose,
trying to channel the sexual energy
of a self-propelled missile, 'Keep on moving.'

The dread swished around my gums
like someone else's tongue. If I had owned a penis
it would've secretly shrivelled in my pants.
'We've passed this clearing before,' Nancy said.

'Different clearing,' I said. 'Those are our footprints
from four days ago,' she said. 'Different footprints,' I said.
Then we saw the torpedo. Nancy laughed.
'I suppose you're going to tell me that's a different torpedo?'

It was getting dark and cold. 'I love you. I just love you
so much,' I said, as Nancy remounted, hugging it
and whispering into its back, her mouth almost kissing
the metal. That's when I lost it.

'I'M SORRY I'M NOT A FUCKING TORPEDO!'

'I can't… blast through shit I'm
lost and I'm useless and I've got no fucking
idea where I am or what I'm doing. There. I said it.
Go ahead and dump me because I'm a piece of shit.'

There was a long silence.
Nancy straightened her spine like a dressage rider,
looked at me for an age then said,
'How many times do I have to prove it to you?'

'Prove what?' I said. She sighed,
'What could be more useless and impotent
than a dud torpedo in a forest?'

'I don't understand,' I said. She peeled a snail
from its propeller and threw it at me.
'I know exactly who you are,' she said,
slapping the steel, 'you and him
are headed in the same direction.'

'You mean, nowhere?'
She unzipped her trousers and reached down.
Fat tears appeared on her cheeks like rain. I didn't
understand why she was crying.

'You stupid idiot,' she said, her breath
quickening as she rubbed and grinded,
'Can't you see I'm doing this for you?
Can't you see I'm exploding for the both of us?'

Sincerely

Use the word 'befall.' Take away
this netting, these gardening pots
with the drainage holes, these small square
days the size of calendar boxes; how each
sleep scores a line through the last,
thin and unfrayable as an eyelash. Let's not dodge
branches as the forest runs towards us,
mark time by near misses, loves that mend
sure as cuts sliced through shadow
by a waving hand. I'm done with healing
over like water heals above a sinking body.

Checkout

I think 'so, this is death' and wonder why
I can still see through my eyes. An angel
approaches with a feedback form asking
how I'd rate my life (very good, good,
average, bad, very bad) and I intend to tick
'average' followed by a rant then I recall
your face like a cartoon treasure chest
glowing with gold light, tick 'very good,'
and in the comment box below I write
'nice job.' The angel asks if I enjoyed
my stay and I say 'Oh yes, I'd definitely
come again' and he gives me a soft look
meaning 'that won't be possible but thanks
all the same,' clicks his pen and vanishes.

Temporary Vows

I hold two fingers to my head,
trigger my thumb, I say pow.
I slice my throat with a single stroke,
pull an invisible blade
vertically along my vein.
Remember the deaths we did together?
Twiddling oven knobs in the air
then thrusting our chins to inhale?
I loved you so much
during that experimental play
when you slowly leant forward to nick
your femoral artery then quietly
bled out in your seat until curtain call,
blood only we saw.
As well as death, we'd mime marriage.
I'd slide on a spectral ring
and you'd shiver at the thrill
of my thumb and fingertip
sealing the deal for a second till
the thought melted back into your skin.
I am proficient at beginnings,
The Air Year: the anniversary prior to paper
for which ephemeral gifts are traditional.
Only after our rings became solid
silver did they truly disappear.
Now the house is a mime scene.
Mime blood all over the floor,
trodden into carpet fibres,
shirts, bras, dried to an airy crust
under my nails. I slit
my neck at the traffic lights,
pow on the train, I suspend
my non-knife above my head,
'see what you're making me do.'
Red whirls rise from the cuts.

All these huge thoughts come to
nothing. My shadow is
the chalk outline of a woman
who did not jump.

The Red Telephone

When she phoned to say I'm shivering
in the rain you hung up and cried.

When she phoned to say I've popped
a few mystery pills now I'm swaying
on a bridge you said *I wish things were different*
and cried.

When she phoned to say I'm on the floor
and a man dressed as a Centurion is standing
over me holding a cinderblock you said, crying,
thank you for the information.

When she texted to say I'm purplish,
my nose feels like a hole, all I can see is a storm
grate crudded with yellowness behind my eyes you replied
I love you and then you cried.

When she emailed to say
I'm falling asleep with a cigarette in my hand
and my room smells of petrol you typed
god that sounds awful I'm so sorry
then wrote her this poem
whilst crying.

Now her house is burning down and you're still
writing. This poem will not
drop everything, sit up, get up
from this stale sheet and go to her. Look,
it's just sitting here

and when her ghost returns to you in the night
trailing plumes of smoke like various scarfs
crying *Where were you?* Through your tears,
confused, you'll say *but*

you never asked
you never said
you never told me to come.

The Deadness

It's like being a windmill in a vacuum
packed village. Weekends are the worst.
The taste of nothing is like licking dew off plastic.
Floppy soul, they call it. Slack spirit. Neurological
pins and needles. Someone has drilled a hole in the crown
of my head, inserted a funnel, emptied
molten margarine into my plumbing. *Darling, are you listening?*
Did you know same-sex mice can procreate now?
You're already mid-anecdote about a colony of gannets
or a colleague's kidney stone removal. You're stomping
your wet boots, bashing white sprinkles from your hat
but the air hasn't moved in months, either
we're living in separate weathers
or you have fake snow on your coat.

The Ground

You land on a ridge, six-feet down the cliff
and believe you have fallen from the dread
summit and survived, you think,
this is the ground.
until you notice the larks passing at eye level,
drop a cufflink and fall
fifty-feet into the open palm of another ridge,
deeper in, scratched, clothes torn,
you've lost a shoe but you think
this is the ground,
I can bake that lasagne now
till a kite gets snagged in your hair,
your feet meet a plunging carpet
now you're hanging by your necklace
from a branch thinking
this is the ground,
let's buy a puppy
as you sit in your bracken chair,
as you fall in your chair like a lopped flower head
face-planting – *Yes! Ground!* – in a tree,
wind-burnt from momentum, whip-
lashed by your own screams, oops, then oops,
oops, straddling a lamppost, a pillar, a shed, each time
believing *this is the ground,* believing
you've survived, falling, landing, falling out,
who knows how long you've been travelling
down this thing, incrementally, held in the loosening-
tightening fist of a giant with a featureless face.
Thud. *At last*
I can put up that shelf. Make that baby.
You lie and let your bones heal, looking up
at the distance, experiencing plateau
for the first time, cold, hard, real, the opposite
of air. You shake like a prodigal astronaut.
I could build a house on this, you think,
staggering off.

Urban Myth

Do you remember the one about the fighter plane during World War II, riddled with bullets from enemy fire, and the plucky pilot who took five packs of Wrigley's peppermint gum from his pocket and told his crew to chew – 'Chew, Crew!' – so they chewed, ripping strip after strip from their foil sleeves to bung the bullet holes, plugging each perforation with a tooth-marked blob like a wax seal, wet and glistening, stamped with their personal crest. Six lads on the plane, or four, or five. Seven strips per pack – so that's thirty-five pieces of gum, it'd take at least three minutes, or maybe it'd just take a minute, their jaws would ache and they'd be ridiculously minty, smoke and fire out the window, planes spiralling down out of the sky, towards the ocean. I don't even know if that's how planes work, or if gumming punctures keeps you airborne. I guess you can't have all that wind shrieking through it. Well anyway it's not a true story. If it were true, you'd have heard of it, maybe I saw it in a cartoon. I like it because it's literally the only idea I'd have if asked to bung a bullet hole. We played our love like that for a while. Chewing then stoppering. A patch-up job cobbled in mid-air from whatever we had in our pockets at the time, fighting fire with blobs of miscellaneous optimism, aiming only for temporary insulation, to stopper the sky whistling through us, stay airborne, unofficial and miraculous, cork each new wound with a wad of sweetness freshly printed from the panic of our mouths.

The Girl Who Cried Love

The hovel belonging to The High Priestess of Love was even smaller and dirtier than I remembered. It looked like an igloo made from shit. The doormat was a slab of stone with 'welcome' scratched into it with a penknife. It is difficult to make a doormat sound sarcastic. As I stooped to enter, three giant wind chimes the size of trombones clattered stressfully above my head. A needlework sampler in the porch read 'Home is Where the Heart is so Where the Fuck is This?' The cuckoo clock ticked a hair too fast like a cocaine heartbeat. There was an electric under-floor cooling system that kept the carpet permanently cold. 'You're back,' said The Priestess. She snapped open a deckchair for me. I jumped in terror. 'It's just a chair,' she smirked but we both knew she'd done it on purpose. She sat, or swayed, in a child's swing with her legs through the leg-holes. She was tiny. 'You've come for a key?' 'Yes Priestess.' 'To unlock the heart of a beautiful maiden?' 'Yes Priestess.' I sat in the damp deckchair as she swung before me like a rancid pendulum. 'I've given you shitloads of keys. Aren't you bored yet?' 'This is the last one.' 'That's what you always say.' 'This time it's true.' 'You always say that too.' 'I never knew the meaning of love before.' 'And that.' 'I recently learnt a new word: transformative.' 'You have it tattooed on your neck.' 'Do I? I only learnt it two weeks ago!' I tried to look at my neck. 'It's like watching the same play over and over with a slightly older actress in the lead.' She threw me a rusty gold key. I caught it. I felt the blood rushing back. I felt my clitoris stabilise for a moment. 'Till next time, buster' she said. 'There won't be a next time!' we said together in perfect unison. 'Stop it I'm serious!' we shouted. 'Stop predicting my statements!' we shouted. I tried to say something original. 'What else can I trust except my feelings?' I said. I smiled triumphantly. She pressed play on her obscenely huge television. A cartoon squirrel was standing mournfully at the foot of a tree holding an acorn like a skull and soliloquizing: 'What else can I trust except my feelings?' The Priestess switched it off. 'Squirrel Hamlet,' she said. 'Did you create a whole cartoon show just to make that point?' I said. She threw a napkin at me with my question written on it. It fluttered like a boneless bird. She stopped her swing by punching the ground so hard she buried her fist. 'Anchor yourself,' she whispered.

I Am Not a Falconer

I am standing in this field
Holding my glove in the air
Should I whistle?
I can't whistle
Will she get lost?
Take shelter in a charming tree?
It's starting to rain
Is that bad?
This is a woolly glove
Calm down
Falconers are patient
It's very windy
The sky is so big
She could be literally anywhere
Penzance
India
Why did I let her go?
I'm not a falconer!
Do I just keep standing here?
I'd go home and change
Into appropriate footwear
But what if I missed her?
I bet falcons are like Fedex
The second you nip to the loo…
What am I talking about?
A falconer doesn't get antsy
A falconer just knows
I lift my fist higher
If my arm gets tired I'll switch arms
Miss, Miss!
Like I'm asking God a question
Please come back to me
Through the wind and rain
Come back
Even though you're free
I'm drenched
My glove is wrong
And you are not a falcon

The Final Episode

The 18th-century bawd who sells her daughter's virginity
to an Earl. The tired CIA operative who says 'just do it'
then half a village dies. The plantation owner's wife.
The lonely CEO of the pharmaceutical company
who screams like a banshee when an employee's baby
pukes milk on her pantsuit. The detective who clicks
her Zippo underneath the incriminating photo of her boss.
The 'complex' one who lets her servant girl be whipped.
Who dumps the radioactive material in the reservoir.
Who is given a chance to apologise to a crying friend
and instead pauses and says 'fuck off'. Who is unable
to report her violent husband before he murders someone.
Unable to stop the drone pilot from pressing the button.
Scared of losing her promotion. Covers her ears. Utters
lines like 'I believe you are mistaken, my dear' and
'This is above your pay grade, kid, keep your nose out.'
Who says 'Fine! Fucking fine!' when the partner who
loves her but can't live like this anymore says, 'I love you
but I can't live like this anymore.' Who thinks the truth
would spoil everything. Who burns the crucial letter.
Whose cleavage is angry and heaving. Who drinks
miniature vodkas in the hotel bath and nearly drowns.
Who wears her new husband's dead ex-wife's earrings
to the christening. Who can't forgive her stepson
for existing. Who lets the suicide call go to voicemail.
Who walks to the AA meeting, is met at the church gate
by the greeter who says 'welcome' to which she replies
'fuck you creep' and keeps on walking. Who is sick
in the sink. Who suddenly feels the weight of her actions.
Who hyperventilates into a paper bag. Who splashes water
on her face in a public bathroom, glares at the mirror
and says 'Wise up'. Who knows her narrative arc is peaking,
knows there's goodness in her somewhere, the viewers
have glimpsed it in close-ups and now they're halfway
through the final episode and she's got twenty-two minutes

to wrangle a denouement, fall on her dagger, hand over the list, clear her spiritual debt in a single payment. Look at her standing on your porch step, holding out her heart like an injured bird and begging you to ruin her.

Naphthalene Heights

The hotel was called Naphthalene Heights
which I thought was a strange name for a hotel
but the poetry festival had booked me the room so I had no choice.

Besides, apart from the name, it was a completely normal hotel.

You were waiting for me in the lobby. You couldn't speak.

At the end of Alcestis by Euripides, Alcestis is brought back from
the underworld, mute. Her body has resurrected but her voice
remains dead.

'Is that what happened to you?'
You nodded. You still had soil in your hair.

'How did you die? Who killed you?'
We sat down in the bar. You ate a peanut and looked at me.

You were so beautiful I felt a commotion in the pit of my throat
like my words were fighting over you.

'Shall we order?'
There was a Fun Fact section under the children's menu
with colourful lettering inside speech bubbles rising from the mouth
of a cartoon snake.

FUN FACT: *In the past naphthalene was administered orally to kill
parasitic worms in livestock.*

It wasn't a cartoon snake, it was a cartoon worm.

FUN FACT: *When you smell mothballs you are inhaling Naphthalene.*

'Hotel food can be a little bland. We could eat somewhere else?'

You looked at me so sadly I felt continental plates separating
in my forehead. I studied the menu again.

*FUN FACT: Small children are at risk of eating mothballs, because they
look like candy or other treats.*

The food choices were standard.
Burgers, pies, ravioli. You pointed at a photo of a plate
of macaroni cheese then a photo of a glass of wine.
'Great.'

You coughed up a mothball.
It sat on the table between us like a sad, sucked imperial mint.

'Please say something.'
I handed you a pen.
'Write something on a napkin?'
It struck me that you were the death of the world.

I felt a terrible pain. I looked down.

A small hole was forming in my palm like a ghost was driving
a pencil through it.

'What's happening?'

You took my hand and stared at me through its hole.

Tiny holes were forming all over your face.
Pinpricks of light were shining out of you.
I realised 'holy' was a literal term. I didn't want to lose you
to the glare of the scene behind.

I could already see chairs and tables through you.
I could see the bar.
We were half-hotel.

I remembered that night you kissed me
in the car park of The Nobody Inn, you'd said
'In the next world maybe.'

We held our disappearing hands.

Speechless

It is such a relief for the words
they have been holding so much for so long
wrapped in furs like Russian soldiers
vowels crammed like backpacks, their lettered
backs are broken from it
syllables bent from all the shouldering
but tonight all the words left
the house in their thinnest summer
jackets, despite the December cold, they strutted
out with barely a stitch on
now they're shameless on the air, naked as a tune
sung by a sated ghost as she fades
from the drawing room into the bright
life where all business is complete.

The Insurmountables

Let's say
the married man with tears for eyes
made a talisman from a feather and a dead
butterfly
and burnt it in the corner of the garden

and far away, a woman
felt a burning, felt a cloud
pop in her ribs,
a sudden terrifying lightness in her hand;
jolted in her chair
like someone falling in a dream and
her husband said, what's wrong?
and she said

'nothing'

as the wings caught fire
and fire became flight and the dead
butterfly translated into smoke
and something was released back into the wild

and untrained air where love is born
before we take it home.

Circles

A parchment scroll listing your lovable
traits would unravel to the floor for ages

I sketch a cloud on your skin, it appears
in the sky of your head and rains for ages

It's peaceful down here, a compass needle
fluctuating then realigning itself for ages

A world where destinations are reached by
going round and round in circles for ages

Naming a song by listening to muffled steps
on a dance floor above my head takes ages

Feeling the ceiling rooting for us, your legs
tense and you think 'god I'm taking ages'

Considering all the noise in my head, giving
all of my head to someone *should* take ages

When we're old and beauty's embedded in
your face you won't say 'sorry I took ages'

Take all of the time in the world – no, really –
take all my time, all my years and my ages

Rope Bridges

Your land of love consists mainly of rope bridges
criss-crossing the sky like a cat's cradle, strung
between mountains. For each time you've moved on,
'gotten over' something, a rope bridge hangs
as testament, the last remaining thread of a thought.
Some are twenty-five years old, woven from dolls'
hair and nettles. Some are wholesome and beautiful:
vines planted on opposite sides of the river
naturally grown to span the gap and weave together.
Some are elaborate, pre-planned, constructed under
high tension and enshrined with laminated photographs.
The latest is rickety and narrow but you're crossing
in style. I look up from my inflatable raft
to see you gliding above me, passing into a cloud.

Sanity

I do kind gestures. Remove my appendix.
I put my ear to a flat shell and – nothing.
I play the lottery ironically. Get married.
Have a smear test. I put my ear to the beak
of a dead bird – nothing. I grow wisdom
teeth. Jog. I pick up a toddler's telephone,
Hello? – No answer. I change a light bulb
on my own. Organise a large party. Hire
a clown. Attend a four day stone-walling
course. Have a baby. Stop eating Coco-Pops.
I put my ear right up to the slack and gaping
bonnet of a daffodil – . Get divorced. Floss.
Describe a younger person's music taste as
'just noise.' Enjoy perusing a garden centre.
Sit in a pub without drinking. I stand at the
lip of a pouting valley – SPEAK TO ME!
My echo plagiarises. I land a real love plus
two real cats. I never meet the talking bird
again. Or the yawning hole. The panther
of purple wisps who prowls inside the air.
I change nappies. Donate my eggs. Learn
a profound lesson about sacrifice. Brunch.
No singing floorboards. No vents leaking
scentless instructions. My mission is over.
The world has zipped up her second mouth.

Surrealism for Beginners

We're trapped inside a movie. Apparently.
Last month 'the grand secret'
was disclosed to us via these giant faces
in the sky claiming to be 'producers' benevolently
dropping by to let us know we were
characters trapped inside their movie and
that every decision we made from now on
would be 'in the script' and therefore
we shouldn't blame ourselves too much or get
overly self-critical, some of us were villains,
some bit-parts, some heroes, but
everyone was 'necessary' for the story
and important in their own way, then the sky
went blank and everyone turned to each other
and made that sound crowds make
after receiving unexpected news: hubbub
hubbub. 'We're in a movie! Of course!'
People kept shouting. 'It all makes sense now!'
'So that's why my shoes don't come off.'
'So that's why I'm always losing money
on the same horse.' 'So that's why I gel my hair
like a vampire, I *am* a vampire.'
'I knew I looked too young to be a grandma,'
said my grandma, 'What am I? Thirty-eight?'
They all seemed so reassured, so validated.
The next day, they resumed their roles
with gusto. The greengrocer started
throwing apples at children as a gesture
of goodwill and then winking.
My auntie began consciously 'bustling'
through doorways. Tramps cut the fingers
off their gloves, practised saying 'god bless us all'
then coughing in chorus. Nothing really changed
exactly, reality just got more pronounced
like someone underlined the word 'normal'

in our stage directions, you know? But...
I'm not buying it. 'Trapped inside a movie?'
What is this? Surrealism for beginners?
Yes I keep bursting into song
whenever the streetlights come on. Yes
I keep chasing the girl of my dreams
across New York. Yes we walk hand in hand
along the moonlit river as the disembodied
voice of Ella Fitzgerald drifts through
the glowing blossom trees but these are merely
facts and not the whole truth, I don't care
what 'the producers' in the sky say,
they're not in my heart, they don't know
the subtle earthquake of her eyes. I don't
care if there's a script with these lines
written in it, or some douchebags
throwing popcorn at a screen, I can't see
a screen, I can't see anything but her and I
need to tell her how I feel and my boat
leaves in the morning and she is
on the other side of Manhattan.

Rookie

You thought you could ride a bicycle
but, turns out, those weren't bikes
they were extremely bony horses. And that wasn't
a meal you cooked, that was a microwaved
hockey puck. And that wasn't a book that was
a taco stuffed with daisies. What if
you thought you could tie your laces?
But all this time you were just wrapping
a whole roll of sellotape round your shoe and
hoping for the best? And that piece of paper
you thought was your tax return?
A crayon drawing of a cat. And your best friend
is actually a scarecrow you stole from a field
and carted away in a wheelbarrow.
Your mobile phone is a strip of bark
with numbers scratched into it.
Thousands of people have had to replace
their doors, at much expense, after you
battered theirs to bits with a hammer
believing that was the correct way
to enter a room. You've been pouring pints
over your head. Playing card games with a pack
of stones. Everyone's been so confused
by you: opening a bottle of wine with a cutlass,
lying on the floor of buses, talking to
babies in a terrifyingly loud voice.
All the while nodding to yourself like
'Yeah, this is how it's done.'
Planting daffodils in a bucket of milk.

Little Children

Politically they're puritans.
They gasp at nudity like it's 1912.
They're shocked by minor offences
such as chip stealing. 98% possess zero faith
in the concept of rehabilitation for adults.
As far as little children are concerned
forgivable mistakes occur before sixteen,
after that you're on your own. Their stance
against marital infidelity is Victorian and their
position on divorce aligns with the Vatican City.
Nuance is irrelevant to the infant moralist.
They sit in plastic umpire chairs at the dinner table
shouting out unintelligible scores. They're violent.
They'll head-bang a breast or stuff a sticky hand
up a skirt then just amble away
like raging misogynists. They won't even allow
their mothers to bring home a sexy stranger
on a Friday night. They disapprove of drugs
like Tory neighbours. Their standpoint on drunkenness
is predictably brutal, especially for women.
It's like the sixties never happened. They believe
every adult should be locked into a sexless yet eternal
marriage, never slip up or forget
even a lunchbox, and be completely transparent
and open to feedback 24/7. They're hypocrites.
They spy on you in the toilet. Parents aren't permitted
even the smallest private perversion yet a child
can secretly urinate in a drawer for three weeks
until the smell warrants investigation.
Their relentless indignation! Their fascist vision
of the perfect family! Little children are like
the tsarist autocracy of pre-revolution Russia.
Their soft hands have never known work.
Their reign is unearned.

On behalf of my younger self I apologise
to my parents for the simplistic, ill-informed
and ignorant questions I hurled concerning
their romantic and sexual life choices.
How could you do that to dad?
How could you do that to mum?
I was operating under a false consciousness,
responding to an imagined society governed
by laws I'd gleaned from picture books
about tigers coming to tea. I had no right.
No credibility. Imagine bellowing criticism
from the stalls after seeing two minutes of a play!
Imagine expecting universal loyalty whilst flinging
spaghetti hoops at the wall! Imagine having such
confidence in your innate philosophy of love!

We kneel to tie the laces of their unfeasibly tiny shoes.

Emotional Reasoning

THE first time we entered the empty flat we felt nothing, but after learning of the murders, the second time we felt an eerie presence like a military sonar rippling through our ear canals, the memory of blood on the walls, the children's screams, the relentless knife, it was all there embedded in the building so we tore that building down and boy did we feel better, exorcised, even the automated voice of the self-service checkout machine instantly struck a friendlier tone, street kids started selling lemon and wheatgrass muffins from the back of a toy dumper truck, the factory fumes left a taste of burnt cocoa on our tonsils, we were happy

until we heard about the old Glendale place and what old Gregory Glendale had done in there, inside that house, behind that door, what he'd dragged across that linoleum, the hitchhiker, the nun, the stuff in jars (not one of us touched a lick of jam after that news broke), we got sick just thinking his flesh was in our graveyard, decomposing, the dark matter of him passing through our decent worms, we photographed the exhumation for our records, *sicko sicko*, then went back to work

but our carrots and radishes developed these black lesions and the Mayor pointed out that the worms had already eaten Gregory Glendale's face so his face was in our soil, that unrepentant leer stroking the roots of our vegetables so we stopped eating vegetables, tarmacked our gardens which felt right, for a second, it felt right demolishing the underpass also, felt right publicly crushing the car that almost crushed the girl they found wandering in the road with a single ribbon of blood cascading down her leg – she'd been missing so long her dad had buried an empty coffin unaware she was right behind him, in the church, so we tore down the church and the priest went to prison but something was still horribly off

the envelope glue in the post office tasted like ash so we stopped sending Christmas cards, Fiona Feltham took her dog for a walk on the demolition site of the old Anderson estate, the next week he had heartworm, Leptospirosis, the mark of the devil in his yellow eyes. The Wild

Swimming Club was disbanded due to fear of infected animal urine getting in our ducts, our cuts, our innocent mouths, we shamed Fiona Feltham out of town and shot the dog

then the street kids began kennel-coughing on our porches saying 'we feel hot and shivery' as if it was *our* fault, appealing to us with their boiling little hands as if it was *in* them, somehow, the Anderson crime – caught from the rubble of the building by the dog who peed in the river where the street kids swam, and now even the skinny one with the cataracts was using his kaleidoscope eyes to manipulate us, scare us into helping him, *sorry no you can't come in*

we hired private detectives to expose our dead relatives, smashed our grandfathers' urns after learning what we learnt about the boys and the disgusting parties, someone kicked a middle-aged man to death in the TV section of a supermarket during the sales and we didn't stop it because we could tell from his raspy groans what he was

we changed the slogan on our welcome sign from 'scenic fishing town with an artistic heritage' to 'we know what you are,' this became our holy mantra, we whispered it to bonsai trees, gerbils, to ourselves in the mirror while hate-brushing our teeth, even sang a gentler version to our babies 'twinkle twinkle little star how we wonder what you are' and Christ did we wonder especially after that boy was stabbed twenty times in the forest by a twelve year old girl 'looking for his microchip' or some shit she'd learnt in a chat room so we cut off the internet, cut down the forest

still the hateful things kept happening and no one could tell where the hate came from, no one could locate the source. Were we not vigilant? Worthy of some mercy? Some let up? They're filming a documentary now, lean guys in baseball caps chatting like we're friends even though they'll name it 'Shamesville' and paint us as a coven of bitter freaks, brand *us* the source and tear us down – like we haven't suffered enough, like we don't feel an eerie presence in our houses, like we don't know what we are.

Fridge

I hang up the phone – *sorry I'm busy* – to continue
an old conversation in the mirror. I close my eyes at sunset,
picture a previous sunset. So many backward miles
to travel, steps to retrace. I dropped something.
I might end up in the womb, shouting, 'Has anyone
handed in a leather jacket?' My alarm clock is a muttered
confession obscured by loud music, I wake up pleading
'Pardon? Say that again?' My toothpaste tastes of morning
breath. The future smells like my school-friend's house:
incense and hoover bags, toast and cats. I step out
the shower with six-month-old lipstick on my cheek.
I haunt my own home, silent but for the buzzing
of the fridge with the wine in it, with the secret
light no one can see until they open the door.

Anaesthetic

Just one word. Send me one word.
Lozenge.
Any word.
Lysol. Shellac. Ditto.
And I'll feel better
for an hour until the pain comes
back and then I'll need two words.
Any two words.
Dessert fork.
Shipping agency.
Frosty fields. And I'll feel
better for forty-five minutes then
I'll need three words.
I love you.
Boom! I'll feel better for a whole entire day,
just smacked off my face on reciprocation.
Say it again. Say it twice.
'I love you I love you'
is six words. Now pimp it up. Add:
So much. With all my heart. Until I die.
I'll feel better for a minute. Then I'll get itchy.
Sick. Fist-banging on your door
at night demanding words you owe me.
Ten words!
'I can't bear this anymore I'm going crazy without you'.
Say that! I'll scrape
up the butts of old words
from past messages and suck on them
till my lips burn. I'll start asking for
things that don't make sense. Carve
love into my leg! Spray paint the walls of my womb!
Inject me with 'x's! Make my blood read it!
I'll get the twitches. The shakes.
The cold sweats. The dream
where I'm three foot tall whispering 'talk to me'

to a shock of golden curls which slowly turns
to reveal its face looks just
like the back of its head.
But for now I only need
one word.
Rowanberry.
Filament.
Plank.

Flicker

The lie is a portal and the portal opens
with a crunch like a fire exit
and releases me
into an October day so clear
I can read myself by it. Hello
tree. Hello bus. Hello single
strand of hair across my forehead
like a subtle crack in the universe.
Don't look through the crack!
Aren't railings remarkable?
This lamppost is remarkable,
I can swing around it
like Gene Kelly. This dead body
of leaves comes alive under my feet.
I can kick things to life.
Kiss. Be kissed to life. Feel
my pulse, it's back. Let's go
to the fairground. Whoosh!
My goldfish flickers
in her bag like
a wet flame.

Drawn Onward

please love me
a little bit less, I'm standing on your front lawn yelling
for a helicopter, every morning the smell of your perfume gets
thicker, I mistook my heart
and urges for a twin set, the open road needs someone
like me, reversing through hedges
in my partner's world, plenty of others
hold tighter, if I had my own theme park I'd call it
fuck it monkey, I can't unzip this longing
in a service station toilet, strangle my
rising loss, I must stare down my face
in a coke-sugared mirror, spinning candy floss from
the breath of strangers, no images
compete with new ones, not enough oxygen in
old kisses
compete with new ones, not enough oxygen in
the breath of strangers, no images
in a coke sugared mirror, spinning candy floss from
rising loss, I must stare down my face
in a service station toilet, strangle my
fuck it monkey. Can't unzip this longing?
Hold tighter. If I had my own theme park I'd call it
my partner's world, plenty of others
like me, reversing through hedges
and urges for a twin set, the open road needs someone
thicker, I mistook my heart
for a helicopter, every morning the smell of your perfume gets
a little bit less, I'm standing on your front lawn yelling
please love me

The Golden Age

A woman whose name escapes me
was my ultimate role model growing up.
What was her name? You know. You know
who I'm talking about. Whatsherface, with the hair.
Always wore a cravat. Spat olive pits
into a miniscule silver snuff box. You know.
Her catchphrase was 'If it ain't broke
I'm not interested.' You know who I mean.
Bombshell. Sang that famous song.
'Forkful of Nothing' with the Withering Brothers.
Paris. Lots of stuff to do with Paris. Starred
in that sexy movie with Sandra Bee Deloyne,
really controversial at the time, they played
cross-dressing gravediggers who both end up
pregnant by rival dictators. You know the one.
Coined the phrase 'Nope.'
She was married to that gorgeous guy
who chopped his head off accidentally
whilst fixing a ceiling fan. Her father
burnt to death after throwing a Molotov cocktail
at a trampoline. Come on. She built the world's most
impossible hedge maze, all her gardeners
disappeared. Had a tiny dog called Handbag,
kept her house keys in his stomach. In 1916
she met Lenin in a coffee shop in Zurich
and came up with the entire plan for Red October.
You *must* remember her. She invented
the candy necklace. Liked to pose for photos
with an almost imperceptible trickle of blood
dripping from her right lobe like an earring.
It was political. No? Only wore one sock?
Ran for sheriff in Roswell, New Mexico?
Called Picasso a cunt? Spent time in jail
for illegal importation of sealskin?
Her vagina died like a tooth, turned completely black

like a rose dipped in tar? Set up twenty-three
orphanages in Senegal called the…
'Whatshername Foundation' – goddammit!
She threw an entire hayrick at Hitler during a rally.
To this day no one knows how she managed to a)
arrive at the rally with a hayrick and b) single-handedly
throw it from two hundred yards away.
She travelled solo by tandem bike. Only ate stale bread.
Went mad in a secluded condo in Toleto,
snorted a suitcase of benzocaine through
the snapped-off trunk of a porcelain elephant.
You must know who I'm talking about!
Joined a punk nunnery called 'The Sisters of
Ulterior Motive'. Wrote a book about
the psychic healing properties of peanut butter.
Caught herpes from a mountain lion.
Had an illicit thirty-year love affair with the novelist
and antique dildo enthusiast Greta Turner-Blake.
Played scrabble with Trotsky during his exile.
First woman to play the hurdy-gurdy on national television.
First woman to say 'fuck' in a zoo.
Looked great in a straw hat.
Ushered in the dawn of a new era.
I've got a postcard with her face on it
somewhere in this drawer.

Morality Play

She said 'I find it difficult to care about using plastic bags
or burning diesel or eating vast quantities of beef as I'm
still not entirely convinced that any of this is real.' I said,
'You mean climate change?' She said, 'No, the world. I'm
not sure the world is real. Which makes it really hard to
give a shit about recycling.' I said, 'Oh.' She said, 'Because
what am I recycling exactly? Pixels? Images from someone
else's dream? What looks and feels like a plastic bottle is
probably just a speck of data in a video game. Or a cookie.'
'A cookie?' 'Oh I don't know. Each cloud of pollution is
probably just a shadow passing over the sleeping eyelid of
the alien.' 'What alien?' 'The alien whose dream we're in!'
'Then why care about anything,' I said, 'Why care about
children? Or love? Or what you put inside your body?'
She looked at me like I'd lost the plot. 'Love is essential
to the alien's dream,' she said, 'It's how you win the game.'
'Are we in a game or a dream?' I said, flicking a fag-butt
out of the window. 'It's a high stakes dream,' she said,
'A dream with a purpose. You can fail.' 'What's the prize?
How do you win? For all we know it could be recycling.
Recycling could be the key to the whole game,' I said.
'It's not,' she said, 'you know it's not.' I felt like one of us
should shout the word 'morality' around about now but
instead we fell into bed tearing off each other's clothes like
hamburger wrappers, making munching noises.

Afterwards I stared at the ceiling. The lampshades were plastic,
bolted down. Her eyelids flickered in her sleep as if her head was
watching a fireworks display from the balcony of her neck.
I wondered if I was in her dream. A clean version of me
dancing on ice, twirling her across a frozen river, tracing her
name with my skates, saying things right. I realised I didn't
care about anything else in the world but her. I didn't care
about rising sea levels or polar bears or bees or rainforests
or the death of the sun, it was all just pixels, set design; which

either meant *she* was the true purpose of the alien's dream, the key, or I was unimaginably selfish. In the street below, cars were blowing up. Ash filled the sky like snow. All the badgers had died overnight. I got back into bed but she had died too. I turned my brain off and on again. Then I followed my fag-butt and jumped out the window. On my way down, I got a rush of déjà vu: I had leapt from this hotel before, I recognised the shrill air, the instant blackness. Some fucker was recycling me! As I bled out on the pavement, I thought I heard an alien voice say, 'You've got one life left.'

Prepper

She has not converted a rusty bike into a device
for grinding wheat or sewn a family
of Hazmat suits or built a reinforced steel underground bunker
from the roofs of twenty double-decker buses or decorated her
decontamination room with laminated photos of bygone
natural beauty – sunsets over oceans, children laughing unafraid –
she does not skin roadkill raccoons with a Bantaga knife or clean
her guns over breakfast but my mum is preparing

for the end of the world. She has written her own book of revelations.
It begins 'Expect to outlive them'.
She scrawls my brother's name with a sparkler just to
rehearse his evaporation, stands in the cemetery
of her mind, pre-grieves, seasons plots with tears, graves
so fresh they're still flowerbeds.

It Sneaks Up on You

You determined the exact
position of the stencil. You taped the stencil
to the skyline, dipped your brush in acrylic paint,
wiped it on a paper towel to remove
excess, dabbed along the edges
with light, quick strokes,
angling to prevent bleeding. Patient,
concentrated, your tongue wedged
in the corner of your mouth, until the entire
design was evenly covered.
You rinsed your brushes in a pail
of soapy water, washed the stencil,
took a step back, jumped and screamed
Where the fuck did that come from?

Fancy Dress

A hand in a glove costume
A wife in a traitor costume
A stranger in a hope costume
Your face in a listening costume
An expectant mother in an expectant mother costume
A phone call in a goodbye costume
A plea dressed as an anecdote dressed as a joke dressed
as doesn't matter dressed as never mind
Sex in a conversation costume
A hopelessness dressed as an action dressed as a mouth
dressed as a lie dressed as a confession dressed as bravery
A hopelessness in a bravery costume
A window in a sky poncho
A window holding up a large blue sign
A window getting changed behind a towel made of sky
A wooden table in a family costume
A nightmare in a reality costume
Our reality costumes are really, really good
The Sun rings the Moon's doorbell
Ding-dong. Party!
The Moon says to the Sun, 'What have you come as?'
'Darkness Man!' says the Sun
'Not again,' says the Moon
'By day he's just average Sunny Ray but when night falls he
becomes...'
'It's been 4.5 billion years mate, no one cares about Darkness Man'
'Watch this space'
'That is literally all I ever do'
A sadness in a wit costume
Sad mouths in long flowing robes of laughter
Sad eyes in attention masks
Sad voices in perky fascinators
An unwanted mental image in a physical tick costume
Masturbation in a respite suit
A fall in a getting up again costume

Photographs pretending to be real people smiling at you
The past tarted up like the present
Our present costumes are really, really good
Water in an ice costume (rent only)
Death in a meaning costume
Good lighting in a beauty costume
Infiltration in a giggle costume
A void dressed as a chock-a-block digital calendar complete
with actual appointments and perspiration hairspray
that induces real stress, in a passion hat
A marriage still wearing its passion hat
like a Christmas cracker paper crown on Boxing Day
You in a me costume
Me in a wisdom costume trying to staple the cloak to my skin
An evasion in an answer costume
Time dressed as a decent amount of itself
A closed door in an open door costume
Our open door costumes are really, really good
Have you ever seen a moment in the nude?
Of course not. Moments never remove their costumes
Not even in bed. If you were to see a naked moment
you would be appalled. Their bodies are clammy and vague
like half-finished sculptures. Never let them hold your hand
Their skin is silicone mould. Their palms will retain an imprint
of your fingerprints. Their hand will become yours
Moments are like spies or chameleons
Their voice is the breath that precedes a question that will never
reunite with its words. You wouldn't recognise
a moment outside of this fancy dress party
You'd probably mistake it for a patch of nothingness
'I'm always getting mistaken for a moment,' says the patch
of nothingness, 'It happens at least once a week. Strangers
on the street. Sometimes I'm so exhausted I just go along with it'
Likewise a moment is often mistakenly invited
to talk about nothingness on the radio
Air in a tension costume
Distance in a space between us costume
A little boy in a grown suit wearing old age makeup and liver spots

painted on his hands dressed as my granddad dressed as a final memory
dressed a dying man wearing an it's my time costume
Our letting go costume is biodegradable
and designed to disintegrate after a few wears
4AM in a revelation costume
My face with the horizon drawn across it
A line in an ending costume, brand new, created for the occasion
with this nifty reversible lining, look: just turn inside out
and the ending transforms into the silence that follows

The Tree Room

Splayed out like walruses on the carpet,
we made Christmas decorations
as Cat Stevens sang
from the CD player kindly procured
by the counsellor. It was my first activity.
I'd come straight from detox
to 'The Tree Room' where Carli handed me
a Pritt-stick, two polystyrene balls
and a strip of googly-eye stickers.
Scott was an advertising mogul
for a famous soft drinks company.
He made an angel. *Oh baby baby it's a wild world.*
Carli had three estranged children,
was six weeks sober, bright-eyed and fit,
wore neon sportswear all day
and had long loud conversations
in the telephone-corner at night.
She made an ambitious red nosed reindeer
with pipe cleaner antlers. I remember
how warm it was in there.
I painted the polystyrene balls with glue
then wrapped them in cotton wool.
None of us spoke. I looked at them both,
foreheads furrowed,
glitter pens busy, big legs
tucked sideways beneath them.
My snowman was implausibly fluffy
and his eyes were too far apart
but Carli said 'cute.' I hung him
on a plastic branch. We sat and stared
at our handiwork, knees pulled up
to our chins. *A lot of nice things
turn bad out there.* I know what happened
after they left, the sad
violent details of their respective

returns to the world. I know the storm
I'm shaking with today. But then
we didn't know. *I'll always remember you
like a child, girl.* We were sheltered,
encased, forgiven, reduced
to a communal hum in a room
where our only purpose was to serve,
with childlike industry, the beauty
of a small fake tree.

The Factory Floor

'THINGS HAVE GOT BETTER!' I announced over the tannoy. I'd been guaranteed a huge order and I couldn't wait to put my staff's fears to rest. The effect was instantaneous. I saw the factory floor transform beneath me from a Victorian painting of miserable toil into a bouncing club, modern and sentient. They hugged each other. Threw their caps in the air. Cried like families reunited after a long war. They composed a group song called 'Things have got better'. Looking down from my office window I watched their conga line weave through the drilling machines.

The next day we lost the contract. We were haemorrhaging funds. Pay-cuts were inevitable; mass redundancies. I switched on the tannoy to deliver the difficult truth and yelled, 'FREE MONEY!' The floor fell silent. I slapped my culprit of a mouth, bad mouth. I was cupping their happiness like a ladybird in my hands. No one moved. The foreman texted: 'Sorry boss what do you mean?' 'I mean *precisely* what I said!' my voice boomed out from the speakers, 'From now on if you ever need cash at the weekend, thirty quid for a decent bottle of wine or a cheeky grand for your daughter's wedding, a tenner for sushi – I won't ask questions – just write your name and the desired amount on a piece of paper, pop it in my pigeon hole and I'll transfer the money into your account within 24 hours'. I was surprised by the exactness of my detail. 'FREE MONEY!' It was fun to shout, 'FREE MONEY!' They ran around like children high-fiving each other. They added a verse to their song all about me. It was like watching a hip new musical from the best seat in the house.

Next morning I stepped up solemnly. Time to get real. 'Listen up everyone okay there's no easy way to say this but due to insurmountable financial dif.... FOUR DAY WEEK! WE'RE SWITCHING TO A FOUR DAY WEEK BUT YOUR SALARY WILL STAY THE SAME!' Shit. They were staring up at me with slight concern like picnickers clocking a cloud. Why didn't they believe me? Didn't they like me anymore? I was speaking *on a tannoy*. I was on the top floor. I had my own parking space. How could they doubt the transparency of a glass office? I persevered. 'I know you're probably finding it a bit weird receiving all of this increasingly brilliant news from your boss on a daily basis. It's weird for me too. The truth is… our factory is just unbelievably successful. In fact, our accountant is worried we might have *too much* money'. I felt the air soften. It was like watching a fast motion nature video of a million roses blooming simultaneously.

I became a full-time bearer of good news. For the next three weeks I ran a factory devoted to the manufacture of applause. ROAMING MASSEUSE! CIRCUS TUESDAYS! I only spoke to induce cheering. LIFETIME EMPLOYMENT GUARANTEE! I brought so much sunshine into people's lives my skin blistered. Although the prosecution would later describe this time as a 'manic lying spree', I remember it as my month of magical thinking.

Loveborough

No one dies here or chews their food properly.
We break bread rolls in half and choke until we gulp.
We stay up all night talking animatedly to dial tones.
We hit small children whenever we gesticulate.

Occasionally someone faints and we hold a funeral
then applaud and cheer when they inevitably revive,
shouting 'It's a miracle!' We shout 'miracle' a lot:
when the coffee is drinkable, when the drizzle stops.

No one keeps receipts. Our tenement buildings
are modelled after comfortable Scandinavian prisons
so we get our groceries home delivered,
chill out most of the year, lightly repent.

Everyone has a running machine facing a blue wall.
The most beautiful woman in the world around here
is called Samantha and she loves me. She sent a letter
telling me so. I read it to my cactus and it flowered.

My yearning often paralyses me in my armchair
for entire days, the phone just rings and rings.
Samantha leaves long voicemails screaming 'Wake up!'
petrified I'm dead. She's adorable like that.

I'm an addict. I keep a pill on the roof of my mouth
but never swallow it. I will never swallow it.
No one dies here or grinds their pepper.
We pour peppercorns onto our pasta.

In our crumbling music halls, we sing about finality
and trail off before the last verse, laugh, pour a big wine.
We don't end romances we let them overlap
indefinitely until we forget their names.

Christmas is a shit-show. Everything comes out.
We spend ages stuffing the lies back into ourselves.
Samantha wants to move to a different town.
She says our local traditions are 'enfeebling.'

Our quicksand foot spas. Our seated silent discos.
Our in-house pub crawls (just crawling around a pub.)
Our shame bracelets. She uses 'insidious' five times
in one sentence. She says she could love me forever

if I ran away with her to somewhere bright
with breathable fabrics, without the faces of ex-lovers
plastered on all the billboards plus their phone numbers;
a place where people are allowed to move on

get well, find a different answer to their lives.
'But *I'm* your answer,' I tell her, 'and you're mine.
Why would you want to find an answer that isn't me?'
She sighs and says 'Oh, Caroline' in that hurt twang

like I'm missing the point. I put on 'Suzanne'
by Leonard Cohen but she kicks the record player
shouting 'No! I will not 'touch your perfect body
with my mind'! I want a nourishing relationship!'

then storms out before I can feed her an orange.
I lie beneath the bubbles of my bath all day, breathing
through a curly straw. Samantha's not like the others.
She expects something from me. I wish I knew what.

Primitive Heart

You are the size of an orange seed and
developing a heart. Same, baby, same.
Your pre-heart is made of two tubes
which must fuse together now into one
primitive structure. Tell me about it.
By Friday your neural groove will herald
the beginning of your brain. Snap.
I'm a chickpea, bud, a tadpole,

pre-me. Within a week you'll double
in scope. I can't compete with that level
of personal growth. You'll outdo me, pip.
I'm unfused. Sketchy. Two heart strings
fumbling to combine. I'm not supposed to
dread completion, baby, am I? Yours nor mine.

Acknowledgements

I would like to thank the editors of the following magazines and journals, where some of these poems were first published: 'Temporary Vows', 'Sanity', and 'The Final Episode' in *Poetry Magazine*; 'Fancy Dress' in *Poetry Review*; 'The Ground' in *TLS*.

'Dive Bar' was first published in *Proud*, an anthology of stories and poetry by LGBTQ+ authors.